frazely

Small Talk

(Painfully) Realistic Dialogs in German - Beginner (A1-A2)

written by *Carolin Baller*

By purchasing this book, you support independent publishing.

Thank you.

www.frazely.com

Small Talk: The Art
of Boring Conversations

Small talk. Isn't that boring? Well... yes. Can you avoid it? Well... no. This book is your guide to the "Do you come here often?" moments we all love to hate.

Small talk is a very real and useful tool to take your first steps in a new language. This book will teach you how to introduce yourself, ask basic questions and keep a conversation going, so you can get through small talk painlessly and maybe even have a little fun along the way!

Who is this book for?

Designed to be the first book you ever read in German!

It is written with beginner learners of German (A1 - A2 level) in mind, and contains:

- Only basic vocabulary
- Short sentences
- Context to facilitate understanding
- Full translation

What's in this book?

✓ (Painfully) real-life conversations

You will read over 40 small talk conversations from diverse and realistic settings. It may not be the most exciting thing, but it's definitely useful!

✓ Simple, yet engaging

This book uses simple vocabulary and expressions, and that's exactly what you need when you start learning a language.

✓ Side-by-side translation of the full text

Each conversation includes a complete translation. Sentences are numbered, enabling you to effortlessly locate the corresponding English phrase. Enjoy the pleasure of reading without the need for a dictionary.

Who are the authors?

Hi there, fellow German enthusiast!

We are Frazely - a small start-up comprised of language lovers on a mission to create useful, engaging, high-quality language learning materials.

We firmly believe that language learning can be both **enjoyable and effective**. If you're tired of boring textbooks and complex grammar rules, welcome to the Frazely family!

We sincerely hope you'll enjoy reading this book and wish you every success in your German language journey.

Lots of love,

Frazely Team

PS: We would love to hear from you! Feedback, questions, and even complaints (though we hope there aren't any...) are all welcome at hello@frazely.com.

Contents

1. Gutes Wetter

1 - Guten Morgen.

2 - Guten Morgen. 3 Ist das Wetter nicht toll?

4 - Ja, das stimmt. 5 Es ist warm heute.

6 Und es gibt keine Wolken. 7 Wir haben wirklich einen schönen Sommer.

8 - Ja, finde ich auch. 9 Das Wetter ist gerade echt schön.

10 - Aber nächste Woche soll es sich ändern. 11 Es soll regnen. 12 Es wird kälter.

13 - Das ist schade. 14 Aber Regen ist besser als Hitze. 15 Ich mag es nicht, wenn es zu heiß ist.

16 - Oh, ich mag Regen nicht. 17 Ich finde Hitze besser. 18 Ich mag einen heißen Sommer.

1. Good weather

1 - Good morning.

2 - Good morning.

3 Isn't the weather great?

4 - Yes, it is.

5 It's warm today.

6 And there are no clouds.

7 We really are having a lovely summer.

8 - Yes, I think so too.

9 The weather is really nice at the moment.

10 - But it's supposed to change next week.

11 It's supposed to rain.

12 It's getting colder.

13 - That's a shame.

14 But rain is better than heat.

15 I don't like it when it's too hot.

16 - Oh, I don't like rain.

17 I like heat better.

18 I like a hot summer.

2. Wir kennen uns

1 - Hi, du heißt Dana, richtig?

2 - Ja, das stimmt. 3 Woher weißt du das?

4 - Wir kennen uns. 5 Wir haben uns schon mal unterhalten.

6 - Oh, wann war das? 7 Ich kann mich nicht erinnern.

8 - Das war vor zwei Wochen. 9 Wir waren auf einer Party. 10 Wir kennen beide Erika.

11 - Ah ja, stimmt! 12 Jetzt erinnere ich mich! 13 Entschuldige, dass ich mich nicht direkt erinnert habe.

14 - Kein Problem. 15 Das war eine tolle Party!

16 - Ja, das stimmt!

2. We know each other

1 - Hi, your name is Dana, right?

2 - Yes, that's right.

3 How do you know?

4 - We've already met.

5 We've talked before.

6 - Oh, when was that?

7 I can't remember.

8 - It was two weeks ago.

9 We were at a party.

10 We both know Erika.

11 - Ah yes, that's right!

12 Now I remember!

13 Sorry I didn't remember right away.

14 - No problem.

15 It was a great party!

16 - Yes, it was!

3. Wie alt bist du?

1 - Kann ich dich etwas fragen? 2 Wie alt seid ihr?

3 - Wie alt wir sind? 4 Ich bin 25 Jahre alt. 5 Ich bin die älteste.

6 - Oh, du siehst jünger aus!

7 - Findest du? 8 Ich finde nicht, aber danke!

9 - Und wie alt sind die anderen?

10 - Diana ist 20.

11 - Und wie alt ist Peter?

12 - Er ist 21 Jahre alt. 13 Nein, warte, er hatte gestern Geburtstag. 14 Er ist 22 Jahre alt geworden. 15 Und wie alt bist du?

16 - Ich bin auch 20, wie Diana.

3. How old are you?

1 - Can I ask you something?

2 How old are you?

3 - How old are we?

4 I'm 25 years old.

5 I'm the oldest.

6 - Oh, you look younger!

7 - You think so?

8 I don't see it, but thanks!

9 - And how old are the others?

10 - Diana is 20.

11 - And how old is Peter?

12 - He's 21 years old.

13 No, wait, his birthday was yesterday.

14 He turned 22 yesterday.

15 And how old are you?

16 - I'm also 20, just like Diana.

4. Bitte langsam

1 - Wollen wir Deutsch reden? 2 Ist das ok für dich?

3 - Ja, das können wir machen. 4 Aber kannst du bitte langsam reden? 5 Ich spreche noch nicht so gut.

6 - Natürlich, das kann ich machen. 7 Aber du sprichst schon sehr gut Deutsch!

8 - Oh, ich weiß nicht...

9 - Wie lange lernst du schon Deutsch?

10 - Ich lerne Deutsch seit drei Jahren.

11 Es ist schwer. 12 Aber ich mag die Sprache. 13 Ich gebe nicht auf.

14 - Das ist gut. 15 Es braucht viel Übung, eine neue Sprache zu lernen. 16 Du machst das super!

17 - Danke, das ist nett.

4. Slowly, please

1 - Shall we speak German?

2 Is that okay for you?

3 - Sure, we can do that.

4 But can you please speak slowly?

5 I don't speak it that well yet.

6 - Of course, I can do that.

7 But you already speak very good German!

8 - Oh, I don't know...

9 - How long have you been learning German?

10 - I've been learning German for three years.

11 It's difficult.

12 But I like the language.

13 I'm not giving up.

14 - That's good.

15 It takes a lot of practice to learn a new language.

16 You're doing great!

17 - Thank you, that's nice of you.

5. Warum Deutsch?

1 - Ich wollte dich etwas fragen. 2 Warum hast du Deutsch gelernt?

3 - Meine Schwester ist nach Deutschland gezogen. 4 Das fand ich so cool! 5 Ich habe sie einmal in Köln besucht. 6 Das war ein tolles Erlebnis für mich. 7 Aber ich konnte mich nicht mit ihren Freunden unterhalten.

8 Sie haben nicht viel Englisch gesprochen.

9 Deswegen wollte ich dann Deutsch lernen.

10 - Das ist ein schöner Grund. 11 Wann ist deine Schwester nach Deutschland gezogen?

12 - Das ist jetzt schon zehn Jahre her.

13 - Die Zeit vergeht so schnell...

14 - Oh ja, das stimmt. 15 Seitdem habe ich sie oft besucht. 16 Und jetzt kann ich mit ihren Freunden auf Deutsch reden.

5. Why German?

1 - I wanted to ask you something.

2 How come you've learned German?

3 - My sister moved to Germany.

4 I found that cool!

5 I visited her once in Cologne.

6 It was a great experience for me.

7 But I couldn't talk to her friends.

8 They didn't speak much English.

9 That's why I wanted to learn German.

10 - That's a good reason.

11 When did your sister move to Germany?

12 - It's already been ten years.

13 - Time goes by so quickly...

14 - Oh yes, that's so true.

15 I've visited her a lot since then.

16 And now I can talk to her friends in German.

6. Wie lange wohnst du hier?

1 - Hallo, wie heißt du?

2 - Ich heiße Sarah. 3 Und du?

4 - Mein Name ist Peter. 5 Schön dich kennenzulernen!

6 - Ebenfalls!

7 - Wie lange wohnst du schon hier?

8 - Ich wohne hier erst seit einem Monat.

9 - Echt? Ich wohne hier seit zwei Jahren.

10 - Oh, das ist aber lang! 11 Gefällt es dir gut hier in Berlin?

12 - Ja, ich mag es sehr! 13 Es wird nie langweilig. 14 Wie gefällt es dir?

15 - Mir gefällt es auch sehr gut.

6. How long have you been living here?

1 - Hi, what's your name?

2 - My name is Sarah.

3 And yours?

4 - My name is Peter.

5 Nice to meet you!

6 - Nice to meet you too!

7 - How long have you lived here?

8 - I've only lived here for a month.

9 - Really? I've lived here for two years.

10 - Oh, that's a long time!

11 Do you like it here in Berlin?

12 - Yes, I like it a lot!

13 It never gets boring.

14 How about you?

15 - I like it very much too.

7. Wie heißt du?

1 - Hi!

2 - Hi, ist es okay, wenn wir Deutsch reden?

3 - Ja, klar.

4 - Super, das ist einfacher für mich. 5 Wie geht es dir?

6 - Mir geht es super, und dir? 7 - Mir geht es gut, danke. 8 Wie heißt du?

9 - Ich heiße Paul.

10 - Hallo, Paul. 11 Ich bin Hanna.

12 - Wie war das, Anna? 13 Sorry, kannst du das noch einmal wiederholen?

14 - Es ist Hanna.

15 - Ah, ok, Hanna. 16 Jetzt verstehe ich.

17 Schön dich kennenzulernen.

18 - Ebenso, Paul.

7. What's your name?

1 - Hi!

2 - Hi, is it okay if we speak German?

3 - Yes, of course.

4 - Great, that's easier for me.

5 How are you doing?

6 - I'm doing great, and you?

7 - I'm fine, thank you.

8 What's your name?

9 - My name is Paul.

10 - Hi, Paul.

11 I'm Hanna.

12 - How was that, Anna?

13 Sorry, could you repeat that?

14 - It's Hanna.

15 - Ah, got it, Hanna.

16 Now I understand.

17 Nice to meet you.

18 - Likewise, Paul.

8. Meine Lieblingssprache

1 - Entschuldige, ich spreche kein Englisch.

2 Sprichst du Deutsch?

3 - Ja, ich spreche auch Deutsch. 4 Wir können Deutsch sprechen.

5 - Super, ich habe nämlich nie Englisch gelernt.

6 - Hattest du es nicht in der Schule?

7 - Nein, das gab es damals nicht. 8 Aber ich spreche Türkisch und Niederländisch.

9 Und natürlich Deutsch.

10 - Das ist interessant. 11 Was ist deine Lieblingssprache?

12 - Mh, lass mich nachdenken... 13 Ich liebe Türkisch! 14 Man kann sich mit der Sprache toll ausdrücken.

8. My favorite language

1 - Sorry, I don't speak English.

2 Do you speak German?

3 - Yes, I speak German as well.

4 We can speak German.

5 - Great, because I never learned English.

6 - Didn't you have it in school?

7 - No, I didn't back then.

8 But I speak Turkish and Dutch.

9 And German, of course.

10 - That's interesting.

11 What's your favorite language?

12 - Hmm, let me think...

13 I love Turkish!

14 It's a great language for expressing yourself.

9. Wie geht es dir?

1 - Guten Morgen, wie geht es dir?

2 - Mir geht es gut. 3 Aber ich bin noch etwas müde.

4 - Warum bist du müde?

5 - Ich habe nicht so viel geschlafen. 6 Und ich habe Hunger. 7 Und wie geht es dir?

8 - Mir geht es auch gut. 9 Und ich habe auch Hunger. 10 Ich habe noch nicht gefrühstückt. 11 Willst du etwas essen?

12 -Ja, gerne. 13 Sollen wir zu dem Café dort drüben gehen? 14 Sie haben leckere Brote.

15 - Das ist eine gute Idee.

9. How are you?

1 - Good morning, how are you doing?

2 - I'm doing well.

3 But I'm still a bit tired.

4 - Why are you tired?

5 - I haven't slept that much.

6 And I'm hungry.

7 How about you?

8 - I'm fine too.

9 But I'm hungry too.

10 I haven't had breakfast yet.

11 Do you want to eat something?

12 -Yes, I'd love to.

13 Shall we go to that café over there?

14 They have delicious sandwiches.

15 - That's a good idea.

10. Geburtstag

1 - Wie alt bist du?

2 - Ich bin 25 Jahre alt. 3 Und wie alt bist du?

4 - Ich bin älter. 5 Ich bin 30 Jahre alt. 6 Ich hatte letzte Woche Geburtstag.

7 - Oh, herzlichen Glückwunsch nachträglich!

8 - Danke schön!

9 - Hast du gefeiert?

10 - Ja, aber nichts Wildes. 11 Ich war mit meinen Freunden essen. 12 Das war schön.

13 - Das klingt toll!

14 - Willst du deinen Geburtstag feiern?

15 - Ja, ich denke schon. 16 Ich will tanzen gehen.

10. Birthday

1 - How old are you?

2 - I'm 25 years old.

3 And how old are you?

4 - I'm older.

5 I'm 30 years old.

6 It was my birthday last week.

7 - Oh, happy belated birthday!

8 - Thank you very much!

9 - Did you celebrate?

10 - Yes, but nothing crazy.

11 I went out to dinner with my friends.

12 It was nice.

13 - That sounds great!

14 - Do you want to celebrate your birthday?

15 - Yes, I think so.

16 I want to go dancing.

11. Arbeit und Studium

1 - Bist du Student?

2 - Nein, ich studiere nicht. 3 Ich arbeite in einem Büro.

4 - Ist es ein guter Job?

5 - Ich kann mich nicht beklagen. 6 Die Kollegen sind nett. 7 Und ich verdiene sehr gut. 8 Und was machst du? 9 Bist du Student?

10 - Ja, ich studiere Jura.

11 - Oh, das muss ja schwierig sein.

12 - Man muss viel lernen. 13 Aber ich finde es sehr interessant.

14 - Das ist gut! 15 Ich finde Jura auch interessant. 16 Aber ich lerne nicht so gerne.

11. Work and study

1 - Are you a student?

2 - No, I'm not studying.

3 I work in an office.

4 - Is it a good job?

5 - I can't complain.

6 My colleagues are nice.

7 And I earn very well.

8 And what do you do?

9 Are you a student?

10 - Yes, I'm studying law.

11 - Oh, that must be difficult.

12 - You have to learn a lot.

13 But I find it very interesting.

14 - That's good!

15 I find law interesting too.

16 But I don't like learning that much.

12. Wohin fährst du?

1 - Hallo Sarah!

2 - Oh, hallo Tom. 3 Ich hab dich gar nicht gesehen. 4 Wie geht es dir?

5 - Mir geht es gut. 6 Und dir?

7 - Mir geht es auch gut. 8 Wohin fährst du?

9 - Ich fahre zu meiner Mutter. 10 Ich besuche sie.

11 - Oh wie schön. 12 Wie geht es deiner Mutter?

13 - Ihr geht es sehr gut. 14 Oh, ich muss hier aussteigen.

15 - Viele Grüße an deine Mutter!

16 - Ich werde es ihr sagen. Tschüss!

17 - Tschau, bis bald.

12. Where are you going?

1 - Hello Sarah!

2 - Oh, hello Tom.

3 I haven't seen you.

4 How are you?

5 - I'm fine.

6 And you?

7 - I'm fine too.

8 Where are you going?

9 - I'm going to see my mother.

10 I'm visiting her.

11 - Oh, how nice.

12 How is your mother doing?

13 - She's doing very well.

14 Oh, I have to get off here.

15 - Give my regards to your mother!

16 - I will. Bye!

17 - Bye, see you soon.

13. Wie war dein Wochenende?

1 - Wie war dein Wochenende?

2 - Mein Wochenende war schön! 3 Ich war wandern. 4 Das hat Spaß gemacht.

5 - Ach, wie toll! 6 Ich finde wandern auch super! 7 Wo warst du denn wandern?

8 - Ich war hier in den Bergen.

9 - Wie schön, ich liebe die Berge! 10 Warst du alleine dort?

11 - Nein, mit einem Freund.

12 - Zusammen macht es noch mehr Spaß!

13 - Das stimmt! 14 Und wie war dein Wochenende?

15 - Meins war gut, aber etwas langweilig. 16 Ich habe viel gelesen und geschlafen.

13. How was your weekend?

1 - How was your weekend?

2 - My weekend was lovely!

3 I went hiking.

4 It was fun.

5 - Oh, how great!

6 I like hiking too!

7 Where did you go hiking?

8 - I was here in the mountains.

9 - How beautiful, I love the mountains!

10 Did you go alone?

11 - No, with a friend.

12 - It's even more fun together!

13 - That's true!

14 And how was your weekend?

15 - Mine was good, but a bit boring.

16 I read and slept a lot.

14. Woher kommst du?

1 - Woher kommst du?

2 - Ich komme aus Australien. 3 - Oh, interessant! 4 Da war ich noch nie!

5 - Und woher kommst du?

6 - Ich komme aus Russland.

7 - Und du wohnst jetzt hier in Deutschland?

8 - Ja, ich wohne hier seit zehn Jahren.

9 - Bist du oft in Russland?

10 - Nein, nicht mehr so oft. 11 Wohnst du auch hier in Deutschland?

12 - Ja, ich bin für mein Studium hier.

13 - Willst du nach deinem Studium zurück nach Australien?

14 - Ich weiß es noch nicht. 15 Ich mag Deutschland, aber ich vermisse auch Australien.

14. Where are you from?

1 - Where are you from?

2 - I'm from Australia.

3 - Oh, that's interesting!

4 I've never been there!

5 - And where are you from?

6 - I'm from Russia.

7 - And you live here in Germany now?

8 - Yes, I live here since ten years.

9 - Do you often go to Russia?

10 - No, not so often anymore.

11 Do you also live here in Germany?

12 - Yes, I'm here for my studies.

13 - Do you want to go back to Australia after yours studies?

14 - I don't know yet.

15 I like Germany, but I also miss Australia.

15. Partygäste

1 - Und wie ist dein Name?

2 - Mein Name ist Tobias.

3 - Hallo Tobias, wohnst du hier?

4 - Nein, ich wohne im Haus nebenan.

5 Wohnst du hier?

6 - Nein, ich bin auch nur ein Gast.

7 - Und wie ist dein Name?

8 - Ich heiße Oliver.

9 - Wie gefällt dir die Party?

10 - Mir gefällt sie gut. 11 Ich habe viel Spaß. 12 Und das Essen ist sehr lecker.

13 Hast du den Salat schon probiert? 14 Er ist sehr lecker.

15 - Ja, der ist von mir!

16 - Oh, wirklich?

17 - Es freut mich, dass er dir schmeckt.

15. Party guests

1 - And what's your name?

2 - My name is Tobias.

3 - Hi Tobias, do you live here?

4 - No, I live in the house next door.

5 Do you live here?

6 - No, I'm just a guest.

7 - And what's your name?

8 - My name is Oliver.

9 - Do you like the party?

10 - I like it a lot.

11 I'm having a lot of fun.

12 And the food is very tasty.

13 Have you tried the salad yet?

14 It's very tasty.

15 - Yes, it's mine!

16 - Oh, really?

17 - I'm glad you like it.

16. Wie war dein Name?

1 - Wie war dein Name? 2 Entschuldige, ich habe ihn nicht verstanden.

3 - Kein Problem, ich wiederhole ihn gerne. 4 Ich heiße Monika.

5 - Hallo Monika, schön dich kennenzulernen!

6 - Es ist auch schön dich kennenzulernen. 7 Dein Name war Karl, oder?

8 - Ja, das ist richtig. 9 Du hast ihn dir richtig gemerkt.

10 - Warst du schon einmal hier?

11 - Nein, es ist das erste Mal. 12 Und du?

13 - Nein, ich auch nicht. 14 Es gefällt mir sehr gut. 15 Es ist ein schönes Kino.

16 - Ja, das finde ich auch.

16. What was your name again?

1 - What was your name?

2 Sorry, I didn't understand it.

3 - No problem, I'm happy to repeat it.

4 My name is Monika.

5 - Hi Monika, nice to meet you!

6 - It's nice to meet you too.

7 Your name was Karl, right?

8 - Yes, that's right.

9 You remembered it correctly.

10 - Have you been here before?

11 - No, it's my first time.

12 And you?

13 - No, I haven't either.

14 I like it though.

15 It's a nice movie theater.

16 - Yes, I think so too.

17. Macht Sport Spaß?

1 - Bist du häufiger hier?

2 - Ja, ich bin jeden Mittwoch hier. 3 Ich liebe Yoga. 4 Und du?

5 - Ich bin nicht so oft hier. 6 Ich versuche es, aber es ist schwer. 7 Ich kann mich nicht motivieren. 8 Es ist irgendwie langweilig.

9 - Das ist schade. 10 Vielleicht ist es nicht der richtige Sport für dich?

11 - Mh, das ist eine gute Frage. 12 Das kann sein. 13 Vielleicht sollte ich mir etwas anderes suchen.

14 - Du findest bestimmt etwas für dich.

15 Sport sollte Spaß machen.

17. Is Sport fun?

1 - Do you come here often?

2 - Yes, I'm here every Wednesday.

3 I love yoga.

4 How about you?

5 - I'm not here that often.

6 I try, but it's hard.

7 I can't motivate myself.

8 It find it somewhat boring.

9 - That's a shame.

10 Maybe it's not the right sport for you?

11 - Hmm, that's a good question.

12 Could be.

13 Maybe I should look for something else.

14 - I'm sure you'll find something that suits you.

15 Sport should be fun.

18. Der Spaziergang

1 - Entschuldigung, ist der Platz noch frei?

2 - Ja, er ist frei. 3 Sie können sich gerne setzen. 4 Ich mache Ihnen Platz.

5 - Danke schön. 6 Ich bin so viel gelaufen! 7 Ich bin sehr müde.

8 - Wie lange sind Sie schon unterwegs?

9 - Ich gehe schon seit zwei Stunden spazieren!

10 - Ja, das ist eine lange Zeit. 11 Gefällt es Ihnen gut hier?

12 - Ja, ich finde es sehr schön! 13 Der See ist fantastisch! 14 Ich liebe die Natur. 15 Und wie lange sind Sie schon unterwegs?

16 - Erst seit einer Stunde, aber ich habe Beinschmerzen bekommen. 17 Deswegen mache ich jetzt eine Pause.

18 - Oh, ja, das ist eine gute Idee.

18. Taking a walk

1 - Excuse me, is this seat still free?

2 - Yes, it's free.

3 Feel free to sit down.

4 I'll make room for you.

5 - Thank you very much.

6 I've walked so much!

7 I'm really tired.

8 - How long have you been walking for?

9 - I've been walking for two hours!

10 - That's a long time.

11 Do you like it here?

12 - Yes, I think it's very beautiful!

13 The lake is fantastic!

14 I love nature.

15 And how long have you been walking?

16 - Only an hour, but my legs hurt.

17 That's why I'm taking a break now.

18 - Oh, yes, that's a good idea.

19. Arbeit

1 - Hallo, erkennst du mich nicht?

2 - Oh, hallo Marco! 3 Ich habe dich gar nicht gesehen. 4 Wie geht es dir?

5 - Mir geht es gut. 6 Ich gehe gerade zur Arbeit.

7 - Was arbeitest du?

8 - Ich arbeite in einem Café.

9 - Oh, wie schön!

10 - Und was machst du beruflich?

11 - Ich bin Polizist.

12 - Oh, das ist sicher spannend!

13 - Ja, manchmal ist es aufregend. 14 Wir müssen aber auch viele Berichte schreiben.

15 Das ist ein bisschen langweilig.

16 - Das kann ich mir vorstellen.

19. Work

1 - Hi, don't you recognize me?

2 - Oh, hi Marco!

3 I haven't seen you.

4 How are you?

5 - I'm fine.

6 I'm just going to work.

7 - What do you do?

8 - I work in a café.

9 - Oh, how nice!

10 - And what do you do for a living?

11 - I'm a police officer.

12 - Oh, that must be exciting!

13 - Yes, sometimes it's exciting.

14 But we also have to write a lot of reports.

15 That's a bit boring.

16 - I can imagine.

20. Wo hast du gewohnt?

1 - Hi, schön dich kennen zu lernen.

2 - Hi, ebenso.

3 - Kommst du aus dieser Gegend?

4 - Ja, ich bin hier aufgewachsen.

5 - Ach toll! 6 Ich finde Hamburg ja sehr schön. 7 Ich wohne gerne hier. 8 - Seit wann wohnst du hier?

9 - Ich bin vor drei Jahren hergezogen.

10 - Wo hast du vorher gewohnt?

11 - Ich habe in Berlin gewohnt.

12 - Oh, spannend, eine große Stadt!

13 - Ja, das stimmt. 14 Aber Hamburg ist ja auch groß.

20. Where did you live?

1 - Hi, nice to meet you.

2 - Hi, likewise.

3 - Are you from this area?

4 - Yes, I grew up here.

5 - Oh great!

6 I think Hamburg is very beautiful.

7 I like living here.

8 - When did you move here?

9 - I moved here three years ago.

10 - Where did you live before?

11 - I lived in Berlin.

12 - Oh, exciting, a big city!

13 - Yes, that's true.

14 But Hamburg is also big.

21. Arbeiten am Wochenende

1 - Seit wann arbeitest du hier?

2 - Oh, lass mich überlegen. 3 Ich bin hier schon seit zehn Jahren.

4 - Das ist lang. 5 Und wie gefällt es dir?

6 - Ich mag die Arbeit sehr. 7 Die Kollegen sind nett.

8 - Wie viele Stunden arbeitest du in der Woche?

9 - Ich arbeite acht Stunden am Tag.

10 - Arbeitest du auch am Wochenende?

11 - Nein, das mache ich nicht mehr. 12 Zu Beginn habe ich das schon ab und an getan.

13 Ich wollte mehr Geld. 14 Aber jetzt mache ich das nicht mehr.

15 - Es ist toll, dass wir so flexibel sein können.

16 - Ja, das stimmt. 17 Das finde ich auch toll.

21. Working at the weekend

1 - When did you start working here?

2 - Oh, let me think.

3 I've been here for ten years.

4 - That's a long time.

5 And how do you like it?

6 - I really like the work.

7 My colleagues are nice.

8 - How many hours do you work a week?

9 - I work eight hours a day.

10 - Do you also work at the weekend?

11 - No, I don't do that anymore.

12 I used to do that from time to time at the beginning.

13 I wanted more money.

14 But now I don't do that anymore.

15 - It's great that we can be so flexible.

16 - Yes, that's true.

17 I think that's great too.

22. Urlaub zu Hause

1 - Wo machst du dieses Jahr Urlaub?

2 - Oh, gute Frage! 3 Ich weiß es noch nicht.

4 Mein Mann möchte nach Italien. 5 Aber wir sind uns noch nicht einig.

6 - Wo möchtest du denn hin?

7 - Ich denke eher an Kanada.

8 - Oh, das ist natürlich weiter weg.

9 - Das stimmt, aber ich wollte dort immer mal hin. 10 Hast du schon Pläne?

11 - Ach, ich bleibe zu Hause. 12 Ich habe keine Lust zu reisen. 13 Zu Hause ist es auch schön.

14 - Ja, das ist auch nicht schlecht. 15 Ihr habt ja auch einen schönen Garten.

16 - Ja, das stimmt. 17 Mein Garten ist toll. 18 Da kann ich mich immer am besten entspannen.

22. Holidays at home

1 - Where are you going on vacation this year?

2 - Oh, good question!

3 I don't know yet.

4 My husband wants to go to Italy.

5 But we haven't decided yet.

6 - Where would you like to go?

7 - I'm thinking about Canada.

8 - Oh, that's quite a bit further away.

9 - That's true, but I've always wanted to go there.

10 Do you already have plans?

11 - Oh, I'm staying at home.

12 I don't feel like traveling.

13 It's nice at home too.

14 - Yes, that's not bad either.

15 You have a nice garden, too.

16 - Yes, that's true.

17 My garden is great.

18 It's always the best place for me to relax.

23. Sprachen studieren

1 - Studierst du auch Wirtschaft?

2 - Nein, ich studiere Fremdsprachen.

3 - Ach, das ist ja interessant! 4 Musstest du bestimmte Sprachen wählen?

5 - Ja, zwei Sprachen. 6 Ich habe Spanisch und Persisch gewählt.

7 - Das ist ja spannend! 8 Kannst du die Sprachen sprechen?

9 - Spanisch kann ich schon ganz gut.

10 Das habe ich schon in der Schule gelernt.

11 Aber Persisch habe ich jetzt erst angefangen. 12 Ich bin noch ganz am Anfang. 13 Aber es macht viel Spaß.

14 Welche Sprachen sprichst du?

15 - Ich spreche nur Deutsch und Englisch.

16 Aber das reicht für Wirtschaft.

23. Studying languages

1 - Are you also studying economics?

2 - No, I'm studying languages.

3 - Oh, that's interesting!

4 Did you have to choose certain languages?

5 - Yes, two languages.

6 I chose Spanish and Persian.

7 - That's exciting!

8 Can you speak those languages?

9 - I can speak Spanish quite well.

10 I've already learned it at school.

11 But I've only just started learning Persian.

12 I'm still at the very beginning.

13 But it's a lot of fun.

14 What languages do you speak?

15 - I only speak German and English.

16 But for economics that's enough.

24. Bei den Eltern wohnen

1 - Wohnst du bei deinen Eltern?

2 - Ja, ich wohne noch bei meinen Eltern.

3 Ich muss Geld sparen.

4 - Ich habe auch lange bei meinen Eltern gewohnt. 5 Ich mochte das. 6 Es hat viele Vorteile, denke ich.

7 - Ja, das sehe ich auch so. 8 Wo wohnst du jetzt?

9 - Ich wohne alleine.

10 - Kannst du dir das leisten?

11 - Ja, die Miete ist nicht so hoch. 12 Aber vielleicht ziehe ich bald mit meinem Partner zusammen. 13 Er hat eine große Wohnung.

14 - Ihr seid nicht verheiratet?

15 - Nein, noch nicht. 16 Aber das kommt bestimmt bald.

24. Living with parents

1 - Do you live with your parents?

2 - Yes, I still live with my parents.

3 I have to save money.

4 - I also lived with my parents for a long time.

5 I enjoyed it.

6 It has a lot of advantages, I think.

7 - Yes, I agree.

8 Where do you live now?

9 - I live on my own.

10 - Can you afford it?

11 - Yes, the rent is not too high.

12 But maybe I'll move in with my partner soon.

13 He has a big apartment.

14 - You're not married?

15 - No, not yet.

16 But I'm sure it will happen soon.

25. Südamerika

1 - Er ist ein Schauspieler. 2 Er kommt aus Südamerika. 3 Warst du schon einmal in Südamerika?

4 - Ja, ich war einen Monat lang in Brasilien.

5 - Oh, spannend! 6 Wie fandest du es dort? 7 Was hast du dort gemacht?

8 - Ich mochte es sehr. 9 Ein sehr interessantes Land. 10 Tolle Strände! 11 Ich habe dort gearbeitet. 12 Warst du schon einmal in Südamerika?

13 - Ich war in Kolumbien. 14 Aber nur für zwei Wochen.

15 - Hast du dort Urlaub gemacht?

16 - Genau, Ich habe dort Urlaub gemacht.

17 Es war fantastisch! 18 Ich würde gerne bald wieder dorthin. 19 Aber die Flüge sind leider so teuer.

25. South America

1 - He's an actor.

2 He's from South America.

3 Have you ever been to South America?

4 - Yes, I spent a month in Brazil.

5 - Oh, exciting!

6 How did you find it there?

7 What did you do there?

8 - I liked it a lot.

9 A very interesting country.

10 Great beaches!

11 I worked there.

12 Have you ever been to South America?

13 - I've been to Colombia.

14 But only for two weeks.

15 - Did you go there on vacation?

16 - Exactly, I went there on vacation.

17 It was fantastic!

18 I would love to go there again soon.

19 But unfortunately the flights are so expensive.

26. Sprichst du Spanisch?

1 - Ich habe gehört, du warst in Spanien?

2 Wie lange warst du dort?

3 - Ja, ich habe dort studiert. 4 Ich war dort für ein Jahr.

5 - Dann sprichst du Spanisch?

6 - Ja, ich kann Spanisch sprechen.

7 Sprichst du auch Spanisch?

8 - Nein, aber ich würde es gerne lernen.

9 Die Sprache klingt sehr schön. 10 Ist es schwer Spanisch zu lernen?

11 - Nein, ich finde, dass man es gut lernen kann.

12 - Wie hast du es gelernt?

13 - Ich habe viele Filme auf Spanisch gesehen. 14 Das hat mir sehr geholfen.

15 - Das ist eine gute Idee! 16 Das muss ich auch versuchen.

26. Do you speak Spanish?

1 - I heard you were in Spain?

2 How long were you there?

3 - Yes, I studied there.

4 I was there for a year.

5 - So you speak Spanish?

6 - Yes, I speak Spanish.

7 Do you also speak Spanish?

8 - No, but I would like to learn it.

9 The language sounds very nice.

10 Is it difficult to learn Spanish?

11 - No, I think it's easy to learn.

12 - How did you learn it?

13 - I watched a lot of movies in Spanish.

14 That helped me a lot.

15 - That's a good idea!

16 I'll have to try that too.

27. Ein schöner Name

1 - Entschuldige, ich habe es eben nicht verstanden. 2 Wie ist dein Name?

3 - Kein Problem, es ging ja sehr schnell.

4 Ich heiße Lisa, und du?

5 - Mein Name ist Katharina.

6 - Das ist ein schöner Name.

7 - Findest du? 8 Ich mag ihn eigentlich nicht so gerne.

9 - Oh, das ist schade. 10 Warum magst du ihn nicht?

11 - Ach, ich weiß nicht. 12 Er ist so lang.

13 Aber ich habe mich daran gewöhnt.

14 Magst du deinen Namen, Lisa?

15 - Ja, ich mag ihn. 16 Er kommt von meiner Oma. 17 Sie heißt auch Lisa.

18 - Oh, wie schön.

27. A nice name

1 - Sorry, I didn't understand that.

2 What's your name?

3 - No problem, it went very quickly.

4 My name is Lisa, and yours?

5 - My name is Katharina.

6 - That's a nice name.

7 - You think so?

8 I don't actually like it that much.

9 - Oh, that's a shame.

10 Why don't you like it?

11 - Oh, I don't know.

12 It's so long.

13 But I've gotten used to it.

14 Do you like your name, Lisa?

15 - Yes, I like it.

16 It comes from my grandma.

17 Her name is Lisa too.

18 - Oh, how nice.

28. Wie war die Arbeit?

1 - Hallo, schön, dass du da bist. 2 Ich war nicht sicher, ob du kommst. 3 Wie geht's?

4 - Gut, aber ich bin etwas müde. 5 Ich komme gerade von der Arbeit.

6 - Du arbeitest als Kellnerin, oder?

7 - Ja, genau, ich bin Kellnerin in einem Café.

8 - Wie war die Arbeit? 9 Hattet ihr viel zu tun?

10 - Ja, heute war viel los. 11 Ich hatte ein bisschen Stress. 12 Wir hatten viele Kunden. 13 Es gab viel zu tun. 14 Aber jetzt habe ich ja frei. 15 Jetzt kann ich mich entspannen.

28. How was work?

1 - Hello, nice to see you.

2 I wasn't sure if you were coming.

3 How are you?

4 - Fine, but I'm a bit tired.

5 I've just come from work.

6 - You work as a waitress, don't you?

7 - Yes, that's right, I'm a waitress in a café.

8 - How was work?

9 Did you have a lot to do?

10 - Yes, it was busy today.

11 I was a bit stressed.

12 We had a lot of customers.

13 There was a lot to do.

14 But now I'm off work.

15 It's time to relax.

29. Sprichst du Französisch?

1 - Kannst du das Buch lesen? 2 Es ist auf Französisch. 3 Sprichst du Französisch?

4 - Ja, ich kann ein bisschen Französisch. 5 Aber ich will noch besser werden. 6 Es ist eine schwierige Sprache. 7 Ich muss noch viel lernen. 8 Kannst du Französisch?

9 - Ich hatte es in der Schule. 10 Aber ich habe alles vergessen.

11 - Das ist schade. 12 Wie lange hattest du es in der Schule?

13 - Vier Jahre.

14 - Oh, das ist lang!

15 - Ja, wir mussten. 16 Ich hätte lieber Niederländisch gelernt. 17 Aber das gab es nicht.

18 - Das ist schade. 19 Eine Sprache zu lernen sollte Spaß machen.

20 - Ja, das finde ich auch.

29. Do you speak French?

1 - Can you read this book?

2 It's in French.

3 Do you speak French?

4 - Yes, I can speak a little French.

5 But I want to get better.

6 It's a difficult language.

7 I still have a lot to learn.

8 Do you speak French?

9 - I had it in school.

10 But I've forgotten everything.

11 - That's a shame.

12 How long did you have it in school?

13 - Four years.

14 - Oh, that's a long time!

15 - Yes, we had to.

16 I would have preferred to learn Dutch.

17 But that wasn't possible.

18 - That's a shame.

19 Learning a language should be fun.

20 - Yes, I think so too.

30. Umziehen

1 - Oh, du ziehst weg? 2 Wohin geht es?

3 - Ich ziehe nach Italien.

4 - Oh wow, spannend! 5 Wieso nach Italien?

6 - Ich habe dort Arbeit gefunden. 7 Und ich liebe das Land einfach.

8 - Das ist toll. 9 Wann geht es los?

10 - Ich bin noch zwei Monate hier. 11 Dann geht das Abenteuer los.

12 - Kennst du jemanden in Italien?

13 - Ja, ich habe einen Freund dort.

14 - Das ist gut. 15 Es ist schwer, neu anzufangen.

16 - Ach, ich finde das okay. 17 Mir fällt es leicht, neue Leute kennenzulernen. 18 Ich freue mich schon!

30. Moving

1 - Oh, you're moving away?

2 Where are you going?

3 - I'm moving to Italy.

4 - Oh wow, that's exciting!

5 Why Italy?

6 - I've found work there.

7 And I just love the country.

8 - That's great.

9 When are you leaving?

10 - I'll be here for another two months.

11 Then the adventure starts.

12 - Do you know anyone in Italy?

13 - Yes, I have one friend there.

14 - That's good.

15 It's hard to start over in a new place.

16 - Oh, I think it's okay.

17 I find it easy to meet new people.

18 I'm looking forward to it!

31. Wo ist das Museum?

1 - Entschuldigung, kann ich kurz stören?

2 - Ja, was gibt es?

3 - Ich suche das Museum. 4 Ist es nicht hier irgendwo?

5 - Ja, das ist richtig. 6 Es ist hinter diesem Gebäude. 7 Dort drüben musst du links abbiegen. 8 Da ist das Museum auch schon.

9 - Du meinst hier nach links?

10 - Ja, genau.

11 - Ich verstehe, danke schön. 12 Warst du schon einmal in dem Museum? 13 Wie ist es?

14 - Ja, ich war schon einmal in dem Museum. 15 Ich fand es gut. 16 Es ist sehr interessant.

31. Where is the museum?

1 - Excuse me, can I interrupt for a moment?

2 - Yes, what is it?

3 - I'm looking for the museum.

4 Isn't it here somewhere?

5 - Yes, that's right.

6 It's behind this building.

7 You have to turn left over there.

8 The museum will be right there.

9 - You mean here to the left?

10 - Yes, exactly.

11 - I see, thank you.

12 Have you ever been to this museum?

13 What's it like?

14 - Yes, I've been to this museum before.

15 I liked it.

16 It's very interesting.

32. Hast du Lust zu reden?

1 - Hast du Lust ein bisschen zu reden?

2 - Ja, wir können gerne reden.

3 - Woher kommst du?

4 - Ich komme aus Dänemark.

5 - Das ist ja interessant! 6 Meine Freundin kommt auch aus Dänemark. 7 Wir fahren immer im Winter dorthin. 8 Wir besuchen dann ihre Familie dort.

9 - Das ist ja ein lustiger Zufall! 10 Und woher kommst du? 11 Kommst du aus Deutschland?

12 - Nein, ich komme aus Peru. 13 Warst du schon einmal dort?

14 - Nein, aber ich würde es gerne einmal sehen. 15 Es soll ja sehr schön sein. 16 Wie lange hast du in Peru gelebt?

17 - Zwanzig Jahre. 18 Also fast mein ganzes Leben lang.

32. Would you like to chat?

1 - Would you like to chat a bit?

2 - Sure, we can talk.

3 - Where are you from?

4 - I'm from Denmark.

5 - That's very interesting!

6 My girlfriend is also from Denmark.

7 We always go there in winter.

8 We visit her family there.

9 - That's a funny coincidence!

10 And where are you from?

11 Are you from Germany?

12 - No, I'm from Peru.

13 Have you ever been there?

14 - No, but I would like to see it sometime.

15 I hear it's very beautiful.

16 How long did you live in Peru?

17 - Twenty years.

18 So almost my whole life.

33. Ich komme hierher

1 - Hallo, wie geht's?

2 - Hallo, gut, und dir?

3 - Mir geht es auch gut. 4 Kommst du aus Deutschland?

5 - Nein, ich komme aus Indien.

6 - Das ist interessant. 7 Dein Deutsch ist sehr gut!

8 - Danke, das ist nett. 9 Kommst du aus Deutschland?

10 - Ja, ich komme hierher, aus Deutschland. 11 Wie lange bist du schon in Deutschland?

12 - Ich bin hier seit einem Jahr.

13 - Dann hast du aber schnell Deutsch gelernt!

14 - Danke, aber ich habe schon in Indien damit angefangen. 15 Ich bin dort zu einer

Sprachschule gegangen. 16 Da habe ich viel gelernt.

33. I'm from here

1 - Hi, how are you?

2 - Hi, good, and you?

3 - I'm fine too.

4 Are you from Germany?

5 - No, I'm from India.

6 - That's interesting.

7 Your German is very good!

8 - Thank you, that's very kind of you.

9 Are you from Germany?

10 - Yes, I'm from here, from Germany.

11 How long have you been in Germany?

12 - I've been here for a year.

13 - You've learned German very quickly!

14 - Thank you, but I've already started in India.

15 I went to a language school there.

16 I've learned a lot there.

34. Es ist schwer

1 - Willkommen in Polen!

2 - Danke, wie lange wohnst du schon hier?

3 - Seit einem halben Jahr.

4 - Wie kommst du mit der Sprache zurecht? 5 Sprichst du gut Polnisch?

6 - Na ja, ich weiß nicht. 7 Ich kann ein bisschen sprechen. 8 Ich verstehe auch viel. 9 Aber es ist schwer. 10 Ich muss noch viel lernen. 11 Sprichst du Polnisch?

12 - Nein, überhaupt nicht. 13 Ich habe gehört, dass es schwer sein soll.

14 - Ja, das kann ich bestätigen. 15 Aber ich mag die Sprache. 16 Und ich mag das Land. 17 Deswegen bin ich hier. 18 Mit der Zeit wird es bestimmt einfacher.

34. It's hard

1 - Welcome to Poland!

2 - Thank you, how long have you been living here?

3 - For half a year.

4 - How are you getting on with the language?

5 Do you speak Polish well?

6 - Well, I don't know.

7 I can speak a little.

8 I also understand a lot.

9 But it's difficult.

10 I still have a lot to learn.

11 Do you speak Polish?

12 - No, not at all.

13 I've heard that it's difficult.

14 - Yes, I can confirm that.

15 But I like the language.

16 And I like the country.

17 That's why I'm here.

18 I'm sure it will get easier with time.

35. Langsamer sprechen

1 - Entschuldige, ich habe dich nicht verstanden. 2 Kannst du das wiederholen?

3 - Entschuldige, ich habe sehr schnell gesprochen. 4 Ich sage es noch einmal langsamer. 5 Ich habe gefragt, ob es dir hier gefällt.

6 - Ach so, ja, es gefällt mir gut. 7 Danke, dass du langsamer sprichst. 8 Das hilft mir sehr. 9 Lass mich überlegen... 10 Ich mag besonders die Menschen. 11 Sie sind alle sehr nett. 12 Sie sind sehr hilfsbereit. 13 Ich fühle mich sehr wohl. 14 Ich habe nur gute Erfahrungen gemacht.

15 - Das freut mich! 16 Ich denke, wir sind sehr freundlich zu Ausländern. 17 Es kommen sehr viele hierher.

35. Speak slower

1 - Sorry, I didn't understand you.

2 Can you repeat that?

3 - Sorry, I was speaking very quickly.

4 I'll say it again more slowly.

5 I asked if you like it here.

6 - Oh, yes, I like it.

7 Thank you for speaking more slowly.

8 That helps me a lot.

9 Let me think...

10 I especially like the people.

11 They are all very nice.

12 They are very helpful.

13 I feel very comfortable.

14 I've only had good experiences.

15 - Happy to hear that!

16 I think we are very friendly to foreigners.

17 A lot of them come here.

36. Warum Arabisch?

1 - Darf ich dich etwas fragen? 2 Wieso lernst du Arabisch?

3 - Ich habe Verwandte, die Arabisch sprechen. 4 Meine Familie kommt aus Ägypten. 5 Deswegen möchte ich das lernen. 6 Mein Opa zum Beispiel spricht nicht gut Deutsch. 7 Ich will mich mit ihm besser unterhalten können.

8 - Das kann ich verstehen. 9 Das ist ein schöner Grund. 10 Wie lernst du Arabisch?

11 - Ich mache online einen Kurs. 12 Und ich übe mit meinen Verwandten. 13 Das funktioniert gut. 14 Kannst du Arabisch?

15 - Nein, überhaupt nicht. 16 Aber ich habe eine Freundin, die kann Arabisch sprechen. 17 Sie kommt aus Syrien.

36. Why Arabic?

1 - Can I ask you something?

2 Why are you learning Arabic?

3 - I have relatives who speak Arabic.

4 My family comes from Egypt.

5 That's why I want to learn it.

6 My grandpa, for example, doesn't speak German well.

7 I want to be able to communicate with him better.

8 - I can understand that.

9 That's a good reason.

10 How are you learning Arabic?

11 - I'm taking an online course.

12 And I practise with my relatives.

13 That works well.

14 Do you know Arabic?

15 - No, not at all.

16 But I have a friend who can speak Arabic.

17 She comes from Syria.

37. Dein Vorname

1 - Wie ist dein Vorname?

2 - Mein Vorname ist Maya.

3 - Und wie ist dein Nachname?

4 - Mein Nachname ist Schuster.

5 - Ist das ein deutscher Name?

6 - Ja, er ist deutsch. 7 Er kommt von meinem Papa. 8 Er ist Deutscher.

9 - Und deine Mutter?

10 - Meine Mama ist in China geboren.

11 - Interessant! 12 Warst du schon einmal in China?

13 - Leider nein. 14 Aber ich würde gerne einmal dorthin.

15 - Ich war dort einmal im Urlaub.

16 - Und wie fandest du es?

17 - Es ist ein interessantes Land. 18 Es ist natürlich sehr groß. 19 Ich kann es nur empfehlen!

37. Your first name

1 - What is your first name?

2 - My first name is Maya.

3 - And what is your surname?

4 - My surname is Schuster.

5 - Is that a German name?

6 - Yes, it's German.

7 It from my dad.

8 He is German.

9 - And your mother?

10 - My mom was born in China.

11 - That's interesting!

12 Have you ever been to China?

13 - No, unfortunately not.

14 But I would love to go there one day.

15 - I was there once on vacation.

16 - And what did you think?

17 - It's an interesting country.

18 It's very big, of course.

19 I can only recommend it!

38. Woher kommen deine Eltern?

1 - Ich wohne seit zehn Jahren in Deutschland.

2 Du kommst auch nicht hierher, oder? 3 Wie lange wohnst du schon in Deutschland?

4 - Doch, ich habe schon immer hier gelebt.

5 Seit meiner Geburt.

6 - Ach so, aber dein Name...

7 - Mein Name ist nicht typisch deutsch, stimmt.

8 Meine Eltern sind vor 30 Jahren hierhergezogen.

9 - Und woher kommen deine Eltern?

10 - Sie sind aus der Türkei hergezogen.

11 - Ach so, dann habt ihr noch Verwandtschaft dort?

12 - Ja, wir haben noch ein paar Verwandte dort.

13 Jeden Sommer fahren wir in die Türkei.

14 Wir besuchen dann unsere Großeltern.

15 - Das ist schön!

16 - Ja, das ist immer eine schöne Reise. 17 Ich besuche meine Familie gerne.

38. Where are your parents from?

1 - I've lived in Germany for ten years.

2 You're not from here either, are you?

3 How long have you been living in Germany?

4 - I have always lived here.

5 Since I was born.

6 - Oh, but your name...

7 - My name isn't typically German, that's true.

8 My parents moved here 30 years ago.

9 - And where are your parents from?

10 - They moved here from Turkey.

11 - Oh, so you still have relatives there?

12 -Yes, we still have a few relatives there.

13 We go to Turkey every summer.

14 We visit our grandparents then.

15 - That's nice!

16 - Yes, it's always a nice trip.

17 I like visiting my family.

39. Nachbarländer

1 - Wollen wir uns unterhalten? 2 Dann können wir unser Deutsch üben.

3 - Ja, das ist eine gute Idee. 4 Lass uns ein bisschen Deutsch reden.

5 - Wie ist dein Name noch gleich?

6 - Ich heiße Louise.

7 - Schön dich kennenzulernen, Louise!

8 - Dein Name war Daniel, richtig?

9 - Ja genau, das hast du dir ja gut gemerkt!

10 - Namen kann ich mir ganz gut merken.

11 - Das ist praktisch. 12 Ich finde das immer schwierig.

13 - Woher kommst du?

14 - Ich komme aus Spanien.

15 - Oh, ein schönes Land! 16 Unsere Länder sind Nachbarn.

17 - Was meinst du? 18 Woher kommst du?

19 - Ich komme aus Frankreich.

20 - Ah, das ist cool.

39. Neighboring countries

1 - Do you want to talk?

2 We could practice our German.

3 - Yes, that's a good idea.

4 Let's speak a little German.

5 - What's your name again?

6 - My name is Louise.

7 - Nice to meet you, Louise!

8 - Your name was Daniel, right?

9 - That's right, you remembered it well!

10 - I'm quite good at remembering names.

11 - That's practical.

12 I always find that difficult.

13 - Where are you from?

14 - I come from Spain.

15- Oh, what a beautiful country!

16 Our countries are neighbors.

17 - What do you mean?

18 Where are you from?

19 - I'm from France.

20 - Ah, that's cool.

40. Hamburg oder Berlin

1 - Wohnst du hier in Berlin?

2 - Ja, ich wohne hier.

3 - Seit wann bist du in Deutschland?

4 - Ich bin seit fünf Jahren in Deutschland.

5 Aber in Berlin wohne ich erst seit einem Jahr.

6 - Wo hast du vorher gelebt?

7 - Vorher habe ich in Hamburg gelebt.

8 - Ah, interessant! 9 Welche Stadt gefällt dir besser?

10 - Mh, gute Frage. 11 Ich glaube, ich finde Berlin besser. 12 Hier ist mehr los.

13 - Ja, das kann ich gut verstehen. 14 Es wird nie langweilig hier! 15 Ich würde auch gerne in Berlin wohnen. 16 Aber ich habe kein Visum. 17 Aber vielleicht klappt es irgendwann.

18 - Ich drücke dir die Daumen.

40. Hamburg or Berlin

1 - Do you live here in Berlin?

2 - Yes, I live here.

3 - How long have you been in Germany?

4 - I've been in Germany for five years.

5 But I've only lived in Berlin for a year.

6 - Where did you live before?

7 - I lived in Hamburg before that.

8 - Ah, interesting!

9 Which city do you like more?

10 - Hmm, good question.

11 I think I like Berlin more.

12 There's more going on here.

13 - Yes, that makes sense.

14 It never gets boring here!

15 I would also like to live in Berlin.

16 But I don't have a visa.

17 But maybe it will work out one day.

18 - I'll keep my fingers crossed for you.

41. Sommerurlaub

1 - Wir haben uns so lange nicht gesehen.

2 Wie war dein Urlaub?

3 - Er war sehr schön!

4 - Wo warst du im Urlaub?

5 - Ich war in Italien. 6 Warst du schon einmal dort?

7 - Nein, ich war noch nie in Italien. 8 Wie ist es dort?

9 - Es ist toll! 10 Ich liebe Italien. 11 Ich fahre jeden Sommer dorthin.

12 - Sprichst du Italienisch?

13 - Na ja, ein bisschen. 14 Ich wäre gerne besser. 15 Warst du auch im Urlaub?

16 - Ja, wir waren mit den Kindern in den Niederlanden. 17 Es war sehr schön.

41. Summer holiday

1 - We haven't seen each other for so long.

2 How was your vacation?

3 - It was very nice!

4 - Where did you go?

5 - I was in Italy.

6 Have you ever been there?

7 - No, I've never been to Italy.

8 What's it like there?

9 - It's great!

10 I love Italy.

11 I go there every summer.

12 - Do you speak Italian?

13 - Well, a little.

14 I'd like to be better.

15 Have you been on vacation?

16 - Yes, we went to the Netherlands with the children.

17 It was very nice.

42. Andere Sprachen

1 - Wollen wir Deutsch reden? 2 Mein Englisch ist nicht so gut.

3 - Ja, gerne.

4 - Sprichst du noch andere Sprachen?

5 - Ja, ich kann auch Spanisch und Portugiesisch.

6 - Ach, das ist toll! 7 Spanisch und Portugiesisch kann ich leider nicht. 8 Ich spreche aber noch Japanisch.

9 - Oh, interessant. 10 Ist das nicht schwer zu lernen?

11 - Ja, es braucht viel Zeit. 12 Aber das ist ok. 13 Mir macht es Spaß. 14 Ich habe ein paar gute Lernmaterialien gefunden. 15 Das ist sehr hilfreich. 16 Damit lerne ich jetzt schneller.

17 - Das ist toll!

42. Other languages

1 - Shall we speak German?

2 My English isn't that good.

3 - Sure, no problem.

4 - Do you speak any other languages?

5 - Yes, I also speak Spanish and Portuguese.

6 - Oh, that's great!

7 Unfortunately, I don't speak Spanish and Portuguese.

8 But I do speak Japanese.

9 - Oh, that's interesting.

10 Isn't it difficult to learn?

11 - Yes, it takes a lot of time.

12 But that's ok.

13 I enjoy it.

14 I've found some good learning materials.

15 That's very helpful.

16 I'm learning faster now.

17 - That's great!

43. Deutscher Name

1 - Wie ist nochmal dein Name?

2 - Ich heiße Maximilian. 3 Aber du kannst mich Max nennen. 4 So nennen mich alle.

5 - Okay, hallo Max. 6 Bist du Deutsch? 7 Dein Name klingt Deutsch.

8 - Ja, das stimmt. 9 Ich komme aus Deutschland. 10 Wie ist dein Name?

11 - Ich heiße Alba.

12 - Schön dich kennenzulernen, Alba! 13 Woher kommst du? 14 Aus Frankreich?

15 - Nein, aus den USA.

16 - Ah, interessant. 17 Gibt es den Namen dort oft?

18 - Gute Frage, ich weiß es gar nicht. 19 Ich glaube nicht.

43. A German name

1 - What's your name again?

2 - My name is Maximilian.

3 But you can call me Max.

4 That's what everyone calls me.

5 - Okay, hello Max.

6 Are you German?

7 Your name sounds German.

8 - Yes, that's right.

9 I'm from Germany.

10 What's your name?

11 - My name is Alba.

12 - Nice to meet you, Alba!

13 Where are you from?

14 From France?

15 - No, from the USA.

16 - Ah, interesting.

17 Is the name common there?

18 - Good question, I actually don't know.

19 I don't think so.

44. Hobbys

1 - Und was machst du so in deiner Freizeit?

2 - Mh, da muss ich nachdenken. 3 Ich weiß nicht. 4 Ich mache eigentlich nichts.

5 - Du hast keine Hobbys?

6 - Mh, nein, ich glaube nicht. 7 Ich arbeite viel. 8 Ich habe keine Zeit für Hobbys. 9 Und du? 10 Hast du Hobbys?

11 - Ich treffe mich gerne mit Freunden.

12 Und ich lese gerne. 13 Und ich gehe gerne ins Kino. 14 Und ich fahre viel Fahrrad.

15 - Das sind aber viele Hobbys!

16 - Ja, es wird nie langweilig. 17 Ich habe nie genug Zeit.

44. Hobbies

1 - And what do you do in your free time?

2 - Hmm, I'll have to think about that.

3 I don't know.

4 I don't really do anything.

5 - You don't have any hobbies?

6 - Hmm, no, I don't think so.

7 I work a lot.

8 I don't have time for hobbies.

9 What about you?

10 Do you have any hobbies?

11 - I like meeting up with friends.

12 And I like reading.

13 I also like going to the movies.

14 And I cycle a lot.

15 - That's a lot of hobbies!

16 - Yes, it never gets boring.

17 I never have enough time.

45. Was studierst du?

1 - Hallo, schön dich kennenzulernen.

2 Studierst du hier?

3 - Ja, ich studiere an der Uni. 4 Du auch?

5 - Ja, ich studiere auch hier. 6 Was studierst du?

7 - Ich studiere Medizin.

8 - Interessant, hat das einen bestimmten Grund?

9 - Meine Eltern sind beide Ärzte. 10 Das war schon als kleines Kind mein Traum.

11 Und was studierst du?

12 - Ich studiere Mathematik.

13 - Oh, das ist sicher schwer. 14 Gefällt es dir?

15 - Ich fand es in der Schule immer einfach. 16 Aber das Studium ist nicht leicht.

17 Aber es gefällt mir trotzdem.

45. What are you studying?

1 - Hello, nice to meet you.

2 Do you study here?

3 - Yes, I study at the university.

4 Are you studying here too?

5 - Yes, I study here too.

6 What are you studying?

7 - I'm studying medicine.

8 - Interesting, is there a particular reason for that?

9 - Both my parents are doctors.

10 It was my dream even as a child.

11 And what are you studying?

12 - I'm studying mathematics.

13 - Oh, that must be difficult.

14 Do you like it?

15 - I always found it easy at school.

16 But studying is not easy.

17 I still like it though.

46. Wie geht es dir?

1 - Hallo Laura.

2 - Hallo Felix. Wie geht es dir?

3 - Mir geht es gut. 4 Aber ich mache mir etwas Sorgen.

5 - Warum machst du dir Sorgen? 6 Ist etwas passiert?

7 - Es geht um meinen Hund. 8 Er ist krank. 9 Ihm geht es nicht gut.

10 - Oh nein, das tut mir leid. 11 Was hat er denn?

12 - Ich weiß es nicht. 13 Vielleicht hat er etwas Falsches gegessen. 14 Er will immer alles essen. 15 Das ist ein Problem.

16 - Oje, das ist nicht gut. 17 Ich hoffe, dass alles gut wird.

18 - Danke, Laura. 19 Das hoffe ich auch.

46. How are you doing?

1 - Hi Laura.

2 - Hi Felix. How are you?

3 - I'm doing well.

4 But I'm a bit worried.

5 - Why are you worried?

6 Did something happen?

7 - It's about my dog.

8 He's ill.

9 He's not feeling well.

10 - Oh no, I'm sorry.

11 What's wrong with him?

12 - I don't know.

13 Maybe he ate something wrong.

14 He always wants to eat everything.

15 That's a problem.

16 - Oh dear, that's not good.

17 I hope everything will be okay.

18 - Thank you, Laura.

19 I hope so too.

47. Wochenende

1 - Hallo, wie geht's?

2 - Gut, gut, und dir? 3 Gibt's was Neues?

4 - Auch, alles gut. 5 Nein, nichts Neues bei mir. 6 Gibt's etwas Neues bei dir? 7 Was machst du am Wochenende? 8 Hast du schon Pläne?

9 - Freitag will ich feiern gehen.

10 - Alleine?

11 - Nein, nein, mit ein paar Freunden.

12 Und du?

13 - Wir wollen in den Park gehen.

14 Unsere Kinder lieben den Park. 15 Das Wetter ist gerade so toll.

16 - Ja, das stimmt. 17 Das ist eine gute Idee. 18 Vielleicht mache ich das auch.

19 Ich muss jetzt leider los, bis dann!

20 - Alles klar, bis nächste Woche!

47. The Weekend

1 - Hi, how are you?

2 - Good, good, and you?

3 Anything new?

4 - I'm good too.

5 No, nothing new with me.

6 Anything new with you?

7 What are you doing this weekend?

8 Do you already have plans?

9 - I want to go partying on Friday.

10 - Alone?

11 - No, no, with a few friends.

12 And you?

13 - We want to go to the park.

14 Our children love the park.

15 The weather is so great right now.

16 - Yes, that's right.

17 That's a good idea.

18 Maybe I'll do that too.

19 I have to go now, see you!

20 - All right, see you next week!

How did we do?

Dearest Reader,

Congratulations on making it to the end! We truly hope you've enjoyed this book and found it helpful.

How did we do? Would you like more content like this? What was your favorite part? We'd love to hear your thoughts and hope you'll take a moment to review our book. We read every review with great joy! You can also reach us via email at hello@frazely.com.

PS. **We have some good news!** We are always busy creating more cool content for you! You'll find your next engaging book on our author's page.

frazely

We hope you've enjoyed this book.
Thank you for trusting our publication.

www.frazely.com

Made in the USA
Monee, IL
11 May 2025

17250900R00059